Beach Please, Meow for Now
Poems By Alicia Wayne

Beach Please, Meow For Now
Copyright 2020 Alicia Wayne

All rights reserved.

This book or any portion thereof may not be reproduced or used in any manner whatsoever without the express written permission of the author except for the use of brief quotations in a book review.

clovercat81@gmail.com

ISBN - 978-0-578-66983-0

Printing in the United State of America

First Edition

For Ryan.
My husband.
My soulmate.
You inspire the poetry I find in life.
I love you.

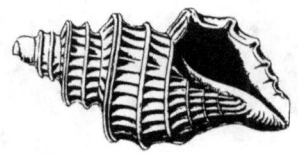

Contents

1. Beginning
2. Nature's Solitude
3. I find you
4. Her Voice Soothed Me
5. Along the Journey
6. Beautiful Place

8. Heartbeat of the Beach
9. Grasping
10. Once Again
11. Moments I Hold Dearly
12. Earthquake
13. Ouija Board
14. Ode to the Pacific Ocean

15. Summer Day of Swimming
17. SPF of my Happiness
18. Sun Setting
19. Morning Walk
20. To Paint
21. A Bright Night
22. Something to Say About It

23. Branching In
24. Summertime Faith
25. Named
26. Silhouette
27. Royal Blue Day
28. Tell Me
29. Aimless Drive
30. Grin
31. Sweet Galaxy
32. Cheers to Fifty Years
33. Where Ivy Still Grows

35. A Moment In Time
36. Aging Gracefully
37. Dreaming
38. Spring in my Step
39. Unquiet
40. In the Cards
41. Wander Lust
42. Rattle
43. Day By Day

Beach Please, Meow for Now

Beginning

Tracing to the roots.
Beginning anew.
Time pauses.
Breathe. In and out.
Steady now, count to four and hold.
Release and repeat.
Calming mind.
Body and spirit match meditative mood.
Cleansing to restart.
All over, again and yet again.
There is beauty in the breaking open of one's heart.
Pouring out pain.
Loving thyself.
Loss becomes gain.

Nature's Solitude

Gazing up through the heather gray marine layer striped sky.
Threaded with palest blue silk,
like gently cascading sunlight.
Get lost in the infinite sky blue abyss.
Deep in thought with new found day dreams.
Cresting upon clouds,
coasting beyond self doubt and destruction.

I Find You

Into the eaves I find you
Hollowed out fears darkening moss
Shifting gray shadowed doubts
Falling away like smoky quartz

Her Voice Soothed Me

Her thick brogue peppered sweet like clovers growing wildly,
tamed with beauty and wisdom.

My Nana, Kathleen Healy Arruda,
had a beautiful Irish accent.

In my girlhood she would sing to me,
and teach me the words.

Oh Danny Boy, My Bonny Lies over the ocean,
and Amazing Grace to name a few.

Endless summer days together,
walking along fields of sunflowers.

Humid evenings stretched out under the late night stars.

We talked, we listened to each other.

Her voice soothed me so, I clung to every single word.

Oh how I would give anything,
to hear my Nana's sweet singing once again.

I hold these memories close to my heart, wrapped with love ,
remembering like yesterday's whispers.

Along the Journey

I write from yesterday to remember tomorrow.
Memories fade into reasons why I love you.
My eyes have seen so many things.
My mind catches up to flickering hopes and dreams.
I recall I always wanted to be a writer when I grew up.
Now I wonder if we ever do really grow up.
Life is a braid with many colors and threads.
The knots and patterns weave into other paths
Along the journey.
I have you in my heart and on my mind.
There are few obstacles on our roads we travel.
Today I write from the present. My past knows
No beginning or end. My soul connects with yours.
And yet, everyday, our journey can begin once again.

Beautiful Place

The stillness of mountain towns.
Earth abounds all of the animal kingdom sounds.
Opalescent sky lifts baby's breath of periwinkle blues.
Marbled cloudy mosaic above creating tie-dyed ocean cruise.
Softly spoken sandy shores inviting me to explore.
Chirping birds calling to their mates.
These are signs of such a beautiful place.

Heartbeat of the Beach

Blanketed obsidian flamed midnight blue
Beckons tranquility
Submerged underwater waves cascading saturation
Liquid forces of mother nature's oceanic beauty
Unleashing turbulent amplified sand
Quiet shore drowning out everything else
Swimming in my ears while floating in my heart
My soul breathes deep the heartbeat of the beach
The ocean sets me free with endless possibilities

Grasping

Grasping to get a hold
of being told and here I am yet again
giving up what was once self control
Keeping track of the fact that I thought I was on a roll
Now back to back nostalgia of the time I sold my soul
Hesitant, not negligent why is this world so incompetent?
Hazards bright and bold-brilliance of the truth
in the fight to uphold
Reliance of the upper hand without a doubt to understand
Living in this land coming undone and unplanned
Crashing down in the lost I am found to impound knowledge
As it all comes around. And around.
Trying to be bold not fitting into the mold
What more can this life unfold?

Once Again

The nerve.
Pain spiraling into the crevices.
Agony filling up and overflowing.
Breaths short and quick. Rapid firing.
Inhaling darts stabbing at a slow moving target.
Sipping tea, molten liquid saturating
to a temporary warming relief.
Only to strike like a cobra in a matter of seconds.
A flaring seared edged sword slicing into my soft gums
between molars.
The cavity screams livid and insidious.
Riveting my mouth with a blast!
Shaking me to tantrum like tendencies.
A week later my dentist performs yet another miracle.
Freeing me from pain once again, for now

Moments I Hold Dearly

Wondering within
Again and again
Trying to place that long-lost friend
Years gone by like a faded blue denim sky
Summertime adventures
New England tides
Humid country roads
Skipping smooth stones
Freshly sweet corn on the cob,
at the court hitting a tennis ball lob
Sunsets at the playground as fireflies blink without a sound
Cookouts in unpredictable downpours
Walking through the mall in all of the air conditioned stores
Jumping off hay stacks on lush evergreen grasses
Running down trails, nearly losing my glasses
These moments I hold so dearly
I hope someday to reunite with my childhood friend
I think of her yearly

Earthquake

Shock waves permeated the ocean floor
Sea life interrupted
Jolting waves upon beached shores
Thundering over and under,
tumultuous and symphonic
Catastrophic occurences blanketed the dot on the map.
The earthquake struck hundreds of miles in the Pacific
and rocked through small towns scattered
upon the Northwest coast.
Shook awake. Electric. Sizzling open fault lines
cracking the earth awake

Ouija Board

Rebelling against youth and all gut instincts,
the Ouija board lured us in
The feel of the planchette beneath sweaty nervous fingertips,
cold to the touch, light as a feather, stiff as a board
Abyss into the unknown,
wandering a fine line between realms
of communication and phantoms
Flirting with paranormal tendencies and morbid curiosity
Limits tested as exploration of the
spirit world heightened our senses
Investigative inquisition sparking spiritualistic awareness
All derived from a "harmless" Parker Brothers game
The game that has no rules
The rules of the otherworldly demons devoid of the unknown

Ode to the Pacific Ocean

A bleak daydream can change course
With infinite possibilities.
The imagination has no shackle, the certainty of the nautilus
has no direct path.
The sea laps away all reason and plan.
I will pour my soul into a meditation of the ocean.
Inspiration floods over me, with waves reaching up to soft
lace clouds.
Sky meets swirls of water. Shamrock green serrated edges
of sharp currents overlap with charcoal blue gray.
I am curious as a cat of the nautical secrets hidden within
the deep sea.
What creatures lurk beneath undisclosed sands?
Salty air breathes life into lungs of hope.
Fresh coldness gently whispers upon my face.
I take in deep breaths of calm. I am an observer of the great
Pacific. It is forever my peaceful place I can go to anytime.

Summer Day of Swimming

Luxury of timelessness.
Reflections danced upon navy blue tiles bordering the pool.
Lost in waves.
Warping sunlight into strange bright shapes.
Smooth rocks nestled underneath the coiled hose were for
throwing into the deep end, and diving in to collect.
I would do this repeatedly, like a dog with a ball.
The cool water comforts refreshed my soul.
Hours would pass as I let the tranquility of the shallow end
cleanse me.
I emptied worries and anxieties that bounced around my
ADD thoughts.
Skimming my hands across the top of the water, I practiced
solo synchronized swimming. Meandering aimlessly, care-
free I would twist my body back and forth
until I was dizzy with exhaustion.
Late afternoons stretched into calm evenings.
Slowly I would finally get out of the pool and dry off.
My body felt like a lullaby after a summer day of swimming.

Spf of My Happiness

Valentine's Day
Upon my face
A walk along the beach
To brighten the sky
The ring on my finger sparkling my mood
The feeling of true love electrifies my inner light
The SPF of my happiness sets record highs!
The beat of my heart is music to my ears

Sun Setting

Looming horizon

As sunset spills across the sky, brilliant colors of twilight
marry the darkening shades of time.

Like watercolors; tangerine flames meet electric coral,
as faded lavender
bleeds into eggplant. Cotton candy bubble gum pink clouds
whisper and float
promises into the night.
My eyes sweep across nature's masterpiece.
Every evening this cycle repeats. Each time a different color
scheme and palate used.
Tomorrow may be crimson waves and mashed potato
clouds with fresh buttery
sunset dripping into the night.
Every evening I become swept away at the beauty that
is dusk kissing night fall hello.

Morning Walk

My eyes feel like Venus flytraps as they pop open awake to take in the serene morning.

Cleansing my face with cool water allows me to gently awaken to the day.

Lacing up my walking shoes, I tread down my driveway, crunching leaves and gravel beneath my feet.

Baby quail run and dart into the bushes where their secret home is beneath the soft ivy leaves.

I stretch, breathing in fresh dawn air, dew drops hydrating the flora and fauna surrounding me, energized by nature.

Submerging my thoughts with positive integrity and true gratitude cleanses my soul, enabling me to start my day with good intentions.

To Paint

I set up my canvas, and lay it on the center of the table.
My brushes and paints stretched out.
All lined up like toy soldiers, ready for combat.
Crimson red, burnt orange, moss green and midnight blue.
All weapons of color; set to light up the blank nothingness.
My landscape comes alive. Awakened with feverish color.
Explosive lavender strokes illuminating the sunset.
Rich panama green highlighting swirls of the sea.
Honeysuckle yellow blending
electric mandarin orange shadows.
Fluorescent pastels lacing the horizon with streamers.
Shocking the sky awake.
Sunset commanding attention to the skyline as vivid technicolor brushstrokes know no boundaries. My colors know no paleness. All is set free from within the depths of my soulful imagination. My mind sets to release all of the vibrant hues of the rainbow.
This is bliss. This is freedom to paint.

A Bright Night

Patterns of moonlight
Illuminate my sight.
Oh, the unquiet night!
How I feel such delight.
Critters that slither.
An owl's wide eyed-
come hither.
Expectations of fright.
My adrenaline putting up
quite a fight.
Bats flying low,
their shrieking makes
my heart drop below.
Adventures in the woods
Mother nature brings her goods.
Midnight sky surrounding me.
Stars glow in silent peace.
Setting me free.

Something to Say About It...

Endless information
Sparking great debates.
Consists of for and foremost
What must be said.
And left unsaid.
Importance of articles for your consideration.
Allotting facts of tallied numbers and lists.
Enabling unwanted advice.
Those protesting freedom of speech.
Quiet untamed minds unleashing words like wildfire.
Hearts on fire worn on sleeves like participation trophies.
Standing in a crowd, high on a soap box.
Ready to fall for it all.
Blissfully well aware.

Branching In

Solace in thoughts.
Intricate patterns of lace webbed together as autumn smoke
deep through whale bone gray birch trees.
Layers of stillness like
paused song
through evergreen leaves.
Mysterious woods
inviting me to be alone.

Summertime Faith

Myriad of contented days filled with uphill climb,
swinging into soulful blue
beyond burgundy maple trees lining t
he perimeters of my imagination.
Suspended somewhere in time,
freshly mowed pastures and jumping off haystacks.
Learning to take one moment and live in it,
and love it wholeheartedly.
Regardless of who is or isn't around,
enjoying long summertime mornings,
stretching into late evenings as sunset
kisses moonlight sky goodnight.
Chasing fireflies by the Atlantic rocky beach
in a small New England town
while sleepy time beckons me
to say my prayers before going to bed.
I have faith in my childhood.
Days of summer linger like promising stars,
brightening my sky of hope.

Named

The titled being
of having a place in the world.
A mark on the Earth.
A stamp in the books.
A film in the capsule.
An engraving on a tombstone.
A tattoo upon the skin.
A portrait over the canvas.
A birth to the life.
A death to the end.

Silhouette

Silhouette
Slipped and set
Arrival approaching
Midnight encroaching
Long lost
At last
Shadows cast
Visionary dreams
Nightfall blankets
Sleeping streams

Royal Blue Day

A kiss of rosy blush upon my cheeks
Opulent sky is a watercolor
painted across the vastness
Royal blue day with black sparrows chirping
Anthem of mid morning

Tell Me

Behind eyes of evergreen and jade,
I wonder what you hide.
Tell me your secrets.
My desire to know is pulling me into a frenzy.
I want to know your everything.
Eyelashes lowered with a sense of mysterious allure.
I yearn to unveil your deepest and darkest

Aimless Drive

The bumps in the road align with listless destination
Curving mountains backdrop forest green redwoods
Aimless drive with nowhere to be
Time suspends into adventure
Heading up highway one
Coasting up the coast
My hands upon the wheel
My heart full of gratitude
Windows open
Sea breezing in
Pulling over on the shoulder
Soft sands beneath my feet
Capturing the stained glass sunset

Grin

Your smile turned grin leaves a thumbprint on my memory
Kindhearted with a laugh erupting from deep in your belly
I think of you and remember you being so easygoing
A genuine happy face, spreading all over and reaching even the corners of your eyes
Your visits were something to look forward to
I hold them close in my heart with my memories of you

Sweet Galaxy

Vast cosmos outward bound
Just beyond the Earth's reach
The universe like an iris kaleidoscope
Whispering unknown oblivion
Surrounding stardust
Orbit my existence

Cheers to Fifty Years

Fifty years! Congrats and cheers!
Love unfiltered through happy tears.
Half a century,
seems like yesterday times infinity so they say!
Romantic and endlessly;
a perfect partnership filled with history.
Faith, honesty, communication and listening
All your beautiful traits I've been witnessing.
I love you both so much Mom and Dad
Your great love story is the truest fairy tale I've ever had

Where Ivy Still Grows

Shining eyes of sweetness
Folded paws tucked under her chin
Adventurous spirit, playful demeanor
Her memories are with us for a lifetime
Her love, like a garden
Where ivy still grows

A Moment of Time

Sometimes I feel like a stuck minute hand on a clock
Paused and hanging in the balance
only temporarily existing
In between shadowed self doubt
Illuminated with hope

Aging Gracefully

Allowing the sun to fill the cracks of age.
Youth radiates ever so slightly;
a diamond with a rough finish and sparkle.
Beneath laugh line sand furrowed brow creases
are dimples of a lingering smile.
Like an etching on a stone, remnants of yesterday's beauty
are aging gracefully.

Dreaming

Moon dusted dreams glitter the night with peaceful sleep.
Time traveling from the pillow to beyond.
Fascination portrays imaginative slumber.
Dead of night becomes alive with fantasy.
Swirling in the mind, unraveling plot twists.
Time to wake up and shake the dreams out.

Spring in My Step

Floral goodness sparkles my well being
Baptized and awash with newness, beginning again
Spring allows regrowth
Blooming open, alive and fresh
Blossoms of petal pink and lavender awakening the quiet streets
Art in nature gives a rejuvenated sense of self

Unquiet

Finding solace in silence
Drinking in the quenching thirst of quiet
Calm and serene waves emptying thoughts
Surrounding me with reflection
Disconnection dissipating
Modern calamity of overly active reactions
Technological tearing apart human connection

In the Cards

If its not "in the cards", then where is it?
Letting the cards fall where they lay seems like
a pointless game of fifty two card pick up.
Cut the deck, then deal the hand.
Will the house always win?
Hands off the cards when the dealer is dealing.
Bless the Tarot deck.
Choose three cards.
Ask a question.
What does the future bring?
The future begins one moment from now.
Shuffle the deck.
And start again.

Wander Lust

I've come down with wanderlust
I can't sit still, so travel I must!
Certainly uncertain of where I wish to go,
so many different destinations allowing to and fro
Behind the wheel and up the coast,
this is the route I love the most
Through redwood coves, on paths of cottage homes,
smoky chimneys
and wood burning stoves
Winding roads leading me right back home
On days in which I yearn to roam

Rattle

Illusion of confusion
Calculated exclusion
Militant and ignorant
Catastrophic grievance
Pledge of allegiance
Factually ineffective, streaming a massive idiot collective
Lost sheep without a shepherd
Misguidance stepped backward
Arming our minds
Ignoring the signs
Unleashing the beast
Crushing chances of peace

Day by Day

Lost in thought
Father time keeping up the pace,
clocking distances between breaths
Day dreaming
Unraveling, unwinding, and letting go
Day by day, the moments that breathe you in

Appreciative Acknowledgements

Thank you to my lovingly patient husband, Ryan.
Your faith in me brought this book to life.

Thank you to my friends. Especially my BFF's:
Natalie, Marianne, and Molly.
You always embrace my creativity.

Thank you to my wonderful parents, Patrick and Maureen.
You instilled in me the values of reading and writing.

Thank you to my entire family. I love you all.

www.ingramcontent.com/pod-product-compliance
Lightning Source LLC
Chambersburg PA
CBHW051412290426
44108CB00015B/2258